Basics and Benefits of Worm Composting:

How to Start With Vermiculture

By David Brian

Basics and Benefits of Worm Composting:

How to Start With Vermiculture

David Brian

Administrator of RedWormFarms.com

Basics and Benefits of Worm Composting:
How to start with vermiculture
Copyright 2020 by David Brian

Publisher: BN Publishing

ISBN 978-7406294608

Table of Contents

FOREWORD

For some years now I have been working on my website RedWormFarms.com (as well as ModelPick.com and WeldingMachineReview.com, my other hobbies apart from the garden) and I very much like writing an article for my sites from time to time.

I enjoy writing about my "Garden Babies" - the red worms or red wigglers.

It is just incredible how helpful they are for your garden!

During this unfortunate Corona Crisis, I had more time than usual and so I decided to put together some of my experiences in this small book that you have bought here. Thank you for that and may you find to love the red worms as much as I do.

David Brian, December 2020

INTRODUCTION AND QUICK START

The proverbial win-win situation is worm composting — also known as vermiculture —. Why?

- It gives you an easy way of disposing of organic waste, such as vegetable peelings.
- It saves landfill space in the county which is good for the environment.
- It provides worms with a happy home, and all the free "eats" they might want.
- The best of all: The homegrown compost is a great way to feed and nurture plants for those who have gardens or even potted plants.

Worm composting, dubbed "the organic garbage disposal" by some advocates, recycles food waste into a rich, dark, earth-smelling soil conditioner. It's such great stuff that Planet Natural offers a variety of organic compost ranging in price from $5.95 to $10.95 as well as compost-containing potting soils. And despite its reputation, worm composting needn't be a smelly effort. If you're careful about setting things upright, your compost bin shouldn't be stinky. Worm composting is increasingly seen as a way of helping our environment and reducing waste. Throughout California, the City of Oakland has a recycling program specifically for food waste. The City of Vancouver in British Columbia, Canada, provides people with worm bins and even has a hotline that you can call to find where to buy worms. Spokane, Washington posts information on how to get started in worm composting to encourage residents to try this eco-friendly garbage disposal.

You need: worms, a container, and a "bedding" to get started.

THE WORMS

Do not go out and dig out night-time crawlers who live by your home in the soil to populate your compost bin. Nightcrawlers must tunnel to eat and survive through dirt and cannot live on vegetable waste. Instead, red-worms are needed — Eisenia foetida (also known as red wiggler, brandling or manure worm), and Lumbricus rubellus (manure worm). You can buy worms from such places as my website RedWormFarms.com or other specialized sites. Sounds a bit strange but yes — it really works, you can order your worms online and they are sent to you by mail. If you have the time and access, you can also find a horse stable and recover worms from horse manure or ask a farmer to ransack his manure pile for worms.

For every pound of food waste per day, Mary Appelh author of "Worms Eat My Garbage" recommends two pounds of worms — about 2,000 wigglers —. (Some experts recommend a one-to-one ratio — one pound of worms per one pound of garbage.) To figure out how much food waste your household generates, monitor it for a week, and divide it by seven. When populating your bin with worms, also keep in mind that worms can double their populations every 90 days, provided you give them adequate food and a good home. It's probably best to start with slightly fewer worms than you need, and just expect your worm population to grow to meet your demand for organic waste processing.

THE COMPOST BIN

The worms will also need a jar. On RedWormFarms.com I have on sale a variety of worm bins including the Wormtopia and the Can O Worms. They are reasonably priced at between USD 100 - 130. You could also create your own if you prefer. When it comes to compost size matters. You're going to want a container that's between 8 and 12 inches deep. Wood is a strong building material. If you don't feel like building from scratch, even a "Rubbermaid" type tub can be adapted and turned into a composting bin. Books like "Worms Eat My Garbage" give you details on how to construct your compost bin. Only note that worms like dark, moist (not wet) environments, and they dislike light. Any container should have an opaque character.

Bins can be found from under the sink outside the kitchen, or in your garage. Temperature is one important consideration. Ideally, a worm compost bin should be located in areas between 40 and 80 degrees Fahrenheit. Red worms generally prefer temperatures of between 55 and 77 degrees. If you live in a harsh winter climate, you'll need to push your bin inside during the winter months, or seasonally composting. Another consideration: worms are like humans because they don't like any noise or vibrations. Keep them away from areas of high traffic.

THE SETUP

You are ready to set up your "compost store" once you have the worms and the containers. First, you want to build your worms a home, and one that will make them happy and productive. You'll need bedding that fills the bin from a third to a half full. Soak up a large quantity of shredded newspapers or cardboard to make bedding. Worms want a 75 % water environment. Newspapers should take just a few minutes to take up enough water to make bedding properly. Allow the cardboard to soak overnight, such as rolls of toilet paper and tissue boxes. Do not use garden soil, or mix in the bedding fresh cow, horse, or chicken manure. These emit gases and will increase your compost bin's temperature. You could have your worms "cooked" to death. Once you have soaked the bedding matter, wring it out until it is moist, but not dripping. Place it with something gritty like a bit of soil, fine sand, leaves, cornstarch, sawdust, or ground eggshells into the bin. (Worms don't have teeth so they need something gritty to help them grind the paper and food.) Once your bin is up and running it will be self-sufficient so you won't need to add any additional grit before you collect the worm castings and clean the bin.

To make your worms feel at home, dig down and place your worms there until about the middle of the bedding. Don't just hang them up. Then put the lid on the bin, keeping it at a moderate temperature. Leave them to settle in alone for about a week. They are going to feed off the bedding.

FEEDING

Start feeding your worms with food scraps like fruit and vegetable peels, pulverized eggshells, tea bags, and coffee grounds after about a week. Avoid meat scraps, bones, fish, leftover dairy products, and oily foods as these will make your pile of compost smell and attract flies and rodents as well. Experts are divided on whether to toss pasta and grains into the compost or throw them away in regular garbage. Your best bet is experimenting and letting your worms tell you what they are going to eat or not eat.

There are certain things of course that worms won't eat or shouldn't eat. Do not dispose of glass, aluminum or plastic foil in your compost. While paper can be used as bedding, don't include colored printed paper on it. The worms are toxic to many colored inks. Eviting rubber bands and sponges too. It is best to feed the worms in small quantities once a week. You will end up with a stinking compost bin when you feed them more than they can handle as the garbage literally back up. Compost does not smell. The foul smell comes from the rotting food which the worms have not yet consumed. If you give them meals of an appropriate size — not supersized entries — they can eat the food before it begins to rot (and smell).

Chop up the vegetable matter if they eat too slowly, which is easier for them to eat and gives new meaning to the term "fast food." If the chopping doesn't help enough, reduce the amount of organic matter you're feeding. When feeding your worms, you can check and see how things are going. Give some extra paper bedding to soak up the excess, if the bedding is wet. (Remember the bedding should be wet, not dripping.) If the bedding is too cold, use spray bottle water to moist it. Once your compost bin is up and running it requires little maintenance until little or no original bedding is visible and the contents of the bin are reduced in bulk and consist mainly of brown and "earthy"-looking worm castings. Once your bin has reached that point it is time to harvest the worm castings and give new bedding to your worms. Between two and a half months to every six months, casts can be harvested anywhere, depending on how many worms you have and how much food you give them.

HARVESTING

There are many different methods of harvesting. For those with the time and patience or small children, you pour the contents of the bin onto a large plastic sheet and then separate the worms from the compost manually. Typically kids love to assist with collecting the worm castings. Remember your helpers should wear gloves as well as yourself. Once all the worm castings have been removed, keep some of the compost aside to mix in with the new bedding and then start the cycle all over again.

A more common way of harvesting is to push everything to one side of the bin - worms, castings, bedding, food. Partially pick up decomposed materials and move to the other side. Put some food over partially decomposed products. Replace the lid, and leave for a few weeks alone. The worms should migrate over into the new food during that time. Put on a pair of gloves once they have gone to the other side, and harvest the castings. Make sure no worms are removed in the process. Then give the worms new bedding with some leftover compost mixed in. Compost is useful whether you have an apartment or a backyard garden adorned with potted plants. Use compost to enrich the potting soil and garden soil. It does a great mulch, too. It's relatively trouble-free and you're not just helping your plants but also the environment.

How to Compost in Wintertime? — Best Options With Worms

Your Options

At some time in the year it's time for us to consider how we can compost our kitchen scraps all year round, especially as fall approaches. To many, living in the world's snowy areas makes it at best impossible to think about composting during the winter. However, when having rich fertilizer ready for your gardening efforts next spring, there are a few things you can do to reduce your landfill footprint year round. Here are just a few different winter composting options:

1. *Indoor compost with worms*
2. *Composting worms outside*
3. *Traditional compost approaches outdoor*

Indoor worm composting is, to me, the best solution for the average household. Many citizens, however, have a decent piece of land to deal with, and maybe a lot of land waste itself. To those occasions, both with and without worms can be composted outdoors with a little extra work during the year.

Worms Composting - Indoors

Let's look at the first option: Worms composting indoors. The first thing you need to get going is a bin for your worms to be living in. You can create several different types of worm bins using nothing more than a rubbermaid bin and a drill. Many, many bins from producers such as the Can-O-Worms, Gusanito Worm Farm, Wriggly Wranch and others are also on the market. These pre-made bins are intended for use indoors; they are nice to look at, relatively easy to harvest from worm castings, and reasonably priced. Personally, I've got my Gusanito bin in my pantry and my worms look awfully healthy. If you choose to build your own indoor worm bin, then this is a simple way to do it. Choose an opaque rubber maid or similar bin; worms don't like the light, and don't like a see-through bin. Drill many holes for drainage along your bin's rim. Using the bin's lid to store any excess liquid. Use small wood blocks or something similar to let the bin rest just one or two inches above the lid; this allows any extra fluid to flow easily out of the bin and into the lid. A worm bin is composed of both bedding materials and worm food materials. After a lot of experimentation I found coconut coir or peat moss to be the best materials to be used as bedding. These materials provide good airflow while at the same time helping to keep flies out, so they are my preference. You can also use shredded paper but I suggest that it be finely shredded before use to help deter pests as well.

So, it's time to make a worm lasagna now that you've got your bin. You're going to add a few inches of moist bedding, dump in a nice pile in your worms, add another inch of moist bedding, add your kitchen scraps, then add two or three more inches of moist bedding. I like the method of lasagna as it facilitates the upward migration of worms to food and helps you to literally lay more food as you go. Sprinkle ground cinnamon generously on top of your top bedding sheet. Cinnamon is a natural insecticide, and will not appeal to flies. This bin I just mentioned is an open device, or a container without a lid. I've found that keeping worms where they belong is simpler if your bins don't have lids. Worm bins with lids also cause condensation along the walls of the interior, which means roaming worms. Even a bin with a lid would provide even less ventilation for your little buddies and they do need to breathe!

Keep a small receptacle near the sink for everyday use, to collect food for your worms. Then, having a larger receptacle in your freezer is wise; this will keep flies away and also help break down the worm food when it thaws. Then, toss the whole contents onto your bin's top layer weekly, and layer again with 3-4 inches of dry bedding. You can thaw the kitchen scraps on the counter and then mix them in a blender or cuisinart if you want to reduce the possibility of flies any further. That makes the waste both easier for the worms to eat faster, and it's also hard for flies to find a nice sticky place to lay their eggs. A well tended washbasin will not be stinky. If you get some unpleasant odors it means you overfed the worms and they cannot keep up. Stop feeding until the smells go away, and it's clear that the worms on the scraps they already have are making good headway.

WORMS COMPOSTING - OUTDOORS

Now let's talk about composting worms outdoors. Thinking that worms can survive an outdoor arctic-like winter may seem insane, but they can certainly do if you give them what they need: warmth and food. First you need to find a place on your property where you'll create a pile of worm compost. You will need to find a good number of straw or hay bales to build the walls of your system after you take a rough measurement (try craigs list). Place them in twos around the edge of your planned worm bed. Then it is time another worm lasagna was made. Start with carton on the ground to serve as a false backdrop to your "pot." And continue to attach layers of yard clippings, leaves, scraps of food and manure. Manure is the main ingredient in a winter worm bed outside, since it produces a lot of heat as it decomposes. Once again, search the craigslist for horse or cow barns in the garden section where you can openly go upload. When the bed is set up, add the worms to it. Drape a black tarp over the entire lot until they have dived deep into the products. The tarp will retain both moisture and gather heat from the sun when it appears in the winter months. If you decide to try a worm bed in winter make sure you have enough worms to process the materials. A good thumb rule is 1 pound per square foot of surface area (though you might get away with less than that). You must also be committed to checking on your worms regularly. Buy a compost thermometer or remote sensor thermometer to make sure the worm bed temperature is about 55-77 degrees Fahrenheit. You can follow the same concept as with composting indoor worms and store your food scraps in the freezer. Then take away the container weekly outside and bury the contents in the existing worm bedding.

There's one special commercial outdoor worm bin for wintertime that I've seen and I have to admit it's fascinating. It is called the Wigwam Worm. This unit is a flow-through system that enables castings to be harvested from the bottom, and it also has a heater that makes it ideal for composting winter worms outdoors. Unfortunately at around $600 it's pretty expensive. If you don't find the cost prohibitive, then give this unit a try anyway.

WINTER COMPOSTING WITHOUT WORMS

Winter outdoor composting without worms can work in much the same way as worms do. You can build the same kind of insulated pile, and be sure to add plenty of manure to heat generation. The only difference is that you will regularly aerate the pile (whereas worms naturally do this). That means you'll need to get bundled up and go out with your shovel at least weekly to manually transform the contents of your pile. Oxygen is required in the decomposition process, so if you want to use this form of pile this is a must-do.

VERY IMPORTANT: EARLY PREPARATION

For any form of composting method, you must plan during the summer / fall to be effective in the winter. Before temperature drops too far, make sure you get your system installed and up and running. Otherwise you may be tempted to just stay in your jammies all winter until spring and forget about the whole composting thing. Yet becoming green is an affair that lasts a year, so be prepared in advance so you can continue to do your part for the environment and produce the organic fertilizer you will need for next year.

Vermicomposting Systems – Additional Guide for a Low Budget Solution

The eisenia fetida or red wiggler worms are among the most underestimated workers in nature. Commonly found in organically rich soils that help to create all over the world including North America and some parts of Europe, these special creatures do something absolutely amazing. In comparison to the normal composting cycle, red worms have become a favorite commodity for organic gardening enthusiasts not only through the worms used to grow their own compost, but also by helping to minimize waste in our landfills while making fresh organic compost at the same time. Here is a really simple device for vermicomposting which anyone can do to build their own worm composting machine.

Organic gardening is gradually becoming one of the most common hobbies not only of enthusiasts for the environment but also of people who happen to boost their health on this natural way. Organic food is known for its ability to retain more nutrients per gram of dry weight of nearly every fruit or vegetable grown in this way. One of the main ingredients is ensuring that sufficient quantities of rich manure are applied to the soil to ensure that the finished product is rich in vitamins, minerals, and phytonutrients that will improve people's overall health by regularly consuming organic food.

Vermicompost or worm compost is an ideal additive for any garden, not only because of the nutrient value but also because of the system that is so easy to set up that almost anyone can use to create their own natural fertilizer. You can take a small container in the form of a box, or a large garbage can and start this composting process, depending on the size of your garden and your needs. The first thing to remember when composting your worm bin is that you need adequate aeration and drainage. Remember that there will be a living population of red worms in your container so it is important to consider their needs. You're going to want to provide fresh air, and also a way for water to flow out so it doesn't stagnate. Essentially, you are building a worker group that can produce a commodity for you, and all they ask is that you regularly feed them from your table with appropriate moisture and ph levels.

There are several types of systems you can try out for vermicomposting, as I have mentioned above already. Some have a constant vertical flow of water and air. These are stacked in the format of trays that our filled from the bottom up on top of each other. The top tray is where you'll put the organic matter the red wigglers are eating and processing. The trays that follow will be used to catch various things like compost, worm castings, and worm cocoons. Building your trays horizontally is also okay but this will take more space, of course. Depending on the scale of your project and the amount of space you have, you might actually build a business of making worm compost with enough organic waste and room to grow in.

Thinking again from the perspective of the worms, you want to create an environment similar to the natural environment used to by the worms in a natural setting. Imagine walking through the forest and considering the underlying temperature of the trees and the layers of leaves that will soon decompose on the forest floor. Similarly, you want a similar soil composition in your bedding as well as an equal temperature so the worms feel like they're in a natural setting and start processing your organic waste. And the bedding will be damp. The bedding materials that you can use to imitate a natural setting would include peat moss, dried manure or even a local store newspaper. The bedding should also allow aeration, so that the process of decomposition and the ability of the worms to access air are available. The temperature should be where humans feel relaxed, or a 60 to 70 ° circle. Finally, the bedding mix needs to have a ratio between carbon and nitrogen so that not only the worms but the other organisms that will live with and help the worms decompose the organic material can feel comfortable. This ratio is approximately thirty to one with most of the bedding content based on carbon, and the rest based on nitrogen.

Once you've thrown all this together that shouldn't take more than a few hours of your time, especially if you have access to the soil and a source for worms, you should start adding organic material to your vermiculture system and letting the process start. One last thing to remember is to protect the worms and their habitat. The most important thing to keep your worm population safe is to ensure it is properly aerated. There needs to be enough oxygen to aerobic rather than anaerobic in their environment. The difference is aerobic which allows the process of decomposition to take place through the worms. Anaerobic is just the opposite and if you left your organic content on your counter for several days or smelled meat rotting, it is close to what you can smell. It is more of a static process while the worms do natural waste processing.

The whole project will cost you no more than $40 to get access to worms and a jar, and a few hours of setup and maintenance time. By doing so, you'll create a small vermicomposting system that will not only produce the freshest compost you'll ever smell but also a rich compost that will add flavor and nutrients to your organic garden goods in a way you've never seen or tasted before.

MOST IMPORTANT BENEFITS OF WORM COMPOSTING

ORGANIC FARMING

The worm casting – especially the one from red worms – contains a higher concentration of macro and micronutrients than the garden compost. It is also enriched with nitrogen, phosphorus, and potassium which are readily available and easily released after the application to the plants and ultimately improve the growth rate of the plants. The vermicompost enhances the plant growth and suppresses diseases of the plant.

IMPROVE SOIL CONDITION

Studies show that, the addition of red worm compost into the soil may improve the biological, structural and physical properties of the soil. They mostly live in top 5" soil because they love to decompose leaves and twig and do not move down deep into the soil. Most of the plants grow in the topsoil. If you apply direct red worm to your garden soil, it increases the porosity and microbial activity in the soil and improves the water holding capacity and aeration in the soil. It also lessens the crusting and other physical damage common to the soil of the arid climate.

Eco-friendly

It also benefits the environment by reducing the amount of chemical fertilizer and pesticides and decreasing the number of wastes going into landfills. The worm will reduce the waste products from kitchen waste. World Bank urban development series of waste composition indicates that on an average about 46% of waste comes from biological means and 25% is particularly from kitchen waste in the form of food. By red worm composting, you can prevent them from ending up in landfills.

Protection of earth from global warming

Research indicated that when your biological waste tossed into landfills upon decomposition it produces methane gas which is 21 times more damaging than carbon dioxide. In this way, landfills are the second-largest producer of methane gas which had a great role in global warming. By using red worm composting you reduce the production of methane and save our earth from global warming effects.

Vermicompost tea

It is a relative by-product of red worm composting, which is a liquid produced by extracting organic matter, microorganisms and nutrients from vermicompost. Studies show it contains 4-5% more nitrogen than the average garden soil but it is slow to release due to mucous secret as they digest the biological waste. Unlike vermicompost, it also applies to the top of plant foliage, reportedly to enhance the disease suppression. Vermicompost tea is also applied to the soil as a supplement between compost application to extend the biological activity.

SUPPLEMENTAL INCOME

If you can rear red worm properly then you can utilize them to form good quality vermicompost for business purposes. You do not need to worry about end suppliers because it includes nurseries, landscape contractors, greenhouses, garden supply stores, flower shops, and the general public.

ECONOMICAL

Using red worms you can form compost in a short period of time. By using it you can physically implement three R (reducing, reusing and recycling) into your lifecycle through red worm composting. It will benefit you financially like:

- It will avoid tipping fees for green waste implemented by many landfills diversion.
- You can make your own nutrient pack organic fertilizer free of cost which costs on average of 50$ per 10pound bag.

CONCLUSION

Have you ever had any very nice soil around your house to garden? Few are. The clay-like soil prevented good water drainage in my case, and was difficult to cultivate new plants. Many times the sand content was too high , causing the opposite problem-accumulation of water. Additionally, there was a lack of a proper soil nutrient for large plants. One could replace all the soil-a time consuming process that is very expensive, build raised beds or work to improve existing conditions. Worm composting is the answer for that. Composting alone is the decomposition of plant remains and other once-living materials to produce an earthy, dirty, crumbly layer that is ideal for adding or enriching garden soil to houseplants. But with the easy help of our little friends it goes faster and gives you a much better quality. Helping the environment is a great way, too. Composting is the process by nature of recycling decomposed organic materials into a rich soil called compost.

Composting is much like cooking, and the easiest compost recipe requires blending parts of green or wet material, high in nitrogen and high in carbon, brown or dry matter. Home composting is both fun and simple to do, and does not require significant time, money and effort investments to be successful. Worm composting is a cheap, natural process that transforms the waste from your kitchen and garden – with the help of your red worms – into valuable food for your garden. Composting is in general a way of reducing the amount of agricultural waste and returning it to soil for the benefit of growing crops.

You will love your garden for it and you will love our little red friends for it, too.

If you need any further information on worm composting and other gardening and composting tips please feel free to consult my website RedWormFarms.com where I will post new articles from time to time.

Other Books by David Brian

Welding Tips & Tricks

Basics and Benefits of Composting

ONE LAST THING...

If you enjoyed this small book or found it useful I'd be
very grateful if you'd post a short review on the website
of your bookseller. Your support really does make a
difference and I read all the reviews personally so I can
get your feedback and make this book even better.

Thanks again for your support!

David Brian

Made in the USA
Monee, IL
07 July 2026